Inbox

Learn how to create & send effective email marketing campaigns.

Copyright © 2012 by 76 Applications Ltd

All rights reserved. No part of this book may be reproduced in any form or by any electronic or mechanical means without permission in writing from 76 Applications Ltd, except for review purposes.

Second edition

For Tony, *my driving force.*

Ingredients

Why email?
Hello… 15
What's so great about email? 17
What's an email
marketing campaign? 21
What makes an effective
email campaign? 23
Your email address 26
Choosing a provider 28

The Plan
Why have a plan? 33
Who's your audience? 35
What's the purpose? 38
List your goals 40
Timeline 41
Measuring the results 43

The right message
Relevance 47
Spam 48
Body works 51
Check it out 53
Links matter 55
Sign your name 57
Subject matters 59
Pre-headers 61

Word play	62
The personal touch	64
Jargon & buzzwords	65
Image ready	67
Attachments	70
On the go	72
Holiday hotspots	74
Track results	75
Social sync	77
Hooks	79
Call to action	81
The legal stuff	82

The right time
There are no experts	87
It's all in the timing	89
Better days	91
Watch the frequency	92

The right people
Buying friends	97
Scraping up	98
Opt-in VS double opt-in	99
The right way	101
Smart segments	104
The email checklist	106

Shameless plug
About Alpha	111
About 76	112

"Give them quality. That's the best kind of advertising."

Milton Hershey

Why email?

Hello…
What's so great about email?
What's an email marketing campaign?
What makes an effective email campaign?
Your email address
Choosing a provider

Hello...

It seems whether you are having a baby or sending an email there's an expert on every TV show, book or website telling you the best way to handle it. Most of this 'expert' advice seem to conflict.

Whilst writing this book we delved into the murky world of stats and facts, looking for some patterns of truth that can once and for all give factual, honest advice to the millions of email marketers around the globe.

Recall the sudden and irrational furore over mad cows disease or the constant 'expert' advice on safe drinking limits or smoking. Although we know deep down there is probably some truth to some of it, we learn to filter it all out. After a while of hearing these messages from different angles - each with different studies, facts and stats - we become hardened to it.

Note this: Most advice you get is from the advisor's own self-interest. Ir's mass market miss-selling. The resulting response is a barrage of advice that becomes watered down and shrugged off.

We've always been told certain rules of thumb when it comes to advertising, but when you start to uncover the real truths you discover the smoke screen of facts were given with a biased viewpoint to back up their own interests.

This book is not designed to give you false facts, nor do we care much for agendas. In fact we've pulled from hard-core studies analysing billions of emails, from reputable companies with no hidden agenda.

We hope you like the book we put together, if so drop us an email with a testimonial and we'll aim to put your comments on our website: inbox@76uk.com

What's so great about email?

Email has been around since MIT (Massachusetts Institute of Technology) developed a way for a single message to be sent from one computer to another. According to Wikipedia the first instance of this dates back to 1965.

Since then, particularly within the last 10-15 years, email has come a long way. It's estimated that there are now over 3.1 billion email accounts that have been created. This is set to rise further over the coming 12 months (2013) to reach 3.6 billion. In fact it's hard to think of the Internet without thinking of email as its primary purpose. Studies found that 83% of people who go online check their emails first before anything else.

Email has become big business. especially SPAM which equates to 81% of all emails sent. That's a lot of businesses (legit or otherwise) trying to make a living using email as their primary marketing tool.

On a personal level, I believe SPAM has become a dirty word, tarnished by the wave of automatically scraped and sent 'dodgy' emails such as Viagra or fake bank login requests. I believe that a legitimate business-to-business email sent for legitimate reasons <u>is not spam</u>.

So, why is email as a marketing medium so popular? First of all, its free to join, it's environmentally green and your customers prefer it. 74% say it's their preferred way of receiving information over text messages, post or phone calls.

From a marketing point-of-view you get great return on your investment. It beats all other mediums. According to a recent survey the following are returns on each dollar spent:

- Email $40.56
- Search engine marketing $22.24
- Internet display advertising $19.72
- Mobile $10.51
- Catalogue $7.30

Plus, you can track the results easily through split testing campaigns, segmenting lists and setting auto-responders.

To top it all off, 36% of consumers say that email marketing has become more relevant in the last 12 months (2012).

So, are you convinced yet?

Why is email a great way to market?

"The first answer is because either nobody is doing it right (and so the few who are doing it right almost have no competition) or because more people are thinking social media is the way to go, and doing little or no email at all. It's kind of like when email first hit the scene. People stopped doing direct mail and so those still doing it cleaned up - since they had so little competition in the mailbox. It's the same with email in a lot of cases.

People think they can just throw up a Facebook fan page or whatever and sales will come in without using boring "retro" email. Of course, the joke is on them - Facebook is not a sales platform and neither is any other social media site."

Ben Settle

What's an email marketing campaign?

An email marketing campaign is much the same as any other marketing campaign, be it flyers, mailshots or networking. These activities are part of your larger marketing strategy. If you have just read the previous chapter then you'll understand that email is not to be ignored.

If you have ever sent an email to a prospective client with the view to getting business then you will have sent an email campaign, chances are, you probably used Gmail, Outlook or your own email service right? Although this is a great place to start, you probably didn't have a way to track the results you got (who clicked, unsubscribed, what bounced, who viewed it in their browser etc). You also probably didn't segment your list, A/B split test or share the email on your social network profiles and pages afterwards. *Did you?*

This book isn't a sales book for Alpha, nor am I going to fill it with jargon – there are guides on the Alpha website for that kind of thing. This book is designed to help you understand the real factors that you need to take into account when sending an email that make a profound difference to your business marketing.

What makes an effective email campaign?

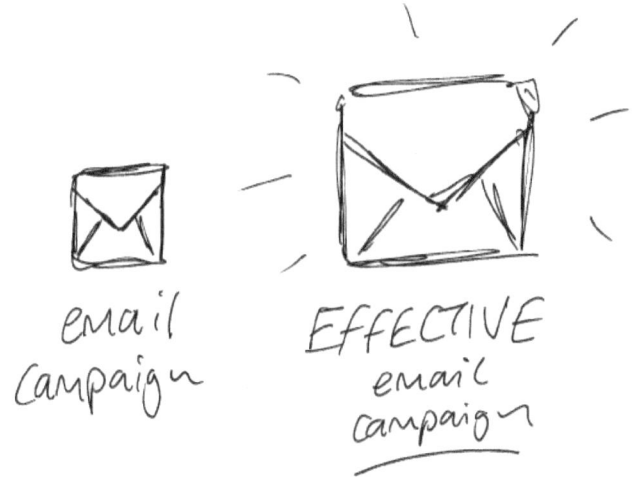

Again there are vast amounts of conflicting data on this, but unlike the stats; they seem to follow a similar pattern.

There are some simple ingredients that once mixed together can produce some amazing results for your business. *Here goes in no particular order:*

- The right message
- The right time

- The right people

Not exactly rocket science is it? You'd think most people understand that a clear message sent out at a time when people are ready to read it and sent to an interested audience is blatantly obvious, yet alas no!

This is where the stats and 'expert' advice comes in. They'll tell you what to write, when to send it and who to send it to. There are teams of people who'd love to grab your hard earned pennies by advising you on 'the right stuff', but quite frankly, it's only you that know who your customers are and what they think. No expert can tell you this.

All an expert can tell you is what books and other experts have told them. It's like Chinese whispers. We're not pretending to be experts, were basing our advise on years of research and facts, with no agenda.

Save yourself a few quid and read this book instead. Better still… send some emails out, learn as you go, get smarter, grab contacts where possible and before long you will be profiting from your email campaigns.

It really is as simple as that. The key is to send, learn, change (*repeat as necessary*).

So you don't feel disheartened by your current campaign results, here are some UK averages to benchmark your next campaign against:

Open rate (the email was read): 18.21%
Click-through rate (someone clicked a link in the email): 3.29%
Unsubscription rate (someone opted-out of your emails): 0.22%

What works and doesn't work?

"It's not about the sender it's about the recipient. It doesn't matter what you want to send them, it matters what they want to read. If you make your messages relevant, give them some value, something that they look forward to receiving, they'll read the messages. When it works for the subscriber, it will work for you."

John Caldwell, Red Pill Email

How effective is email marketing compared with social media, press releases, PPC and other online marketing strategies?

"In my opinion email is an increasingly important part of the marketing mix. Clients spend vast sums of money on acquisition using the above methods and email gives them the opportunity to capture those eyeballs and market to them relatively cheaply."

Mike Parry, Inbox Warriors

Your email address

Most businesses start out with a website. I always recommend a .com if you are a global business - and who nowadays who isn't global with the Internet? If you are locally-focused business then a .co.uk is just fine.

The next logical step is to set up your email address, something like info@yourdomain.com or support@yourdomain.com. However some people continue to use a Gmail or similar address like mybusiness@gmail.com instead - please don't do this! It looks unprofessional. Most web-savvy business owners will know how to create an email account in your domain control panel.

Better still, use your own name in the email address where you can. For example I always use dhugal@76uk.com, not info@... *In fact we don't even have an info@*. Research tells us that recipients of your emails are more likely to read your emails if they come from a person.

When sending email from either your email provider (Gmail, Outlook) or your email campaign sending service (like Alpha) it's a good idea to have an email signature. The signature is a footnote with such things like name, role, email, telephone, web, Skype, Twitter, Facebook, LinkedIn or other social networks. Research also tells us that a simple email signature encourages trust.

Choosing a provider

Now you are one of the 3.6 billion email account holders and are looking for an effective way to market a service or product to some prospective customers, the next logical step is to choose a provider of a professional emailing service.

It's not a good idea to use Outlook or GMail for this purpose for reasons we've covered and there is a tonne of email marketing tools out there. *So, how do you find the right one for you?*

I would love to be biased and tell you Alpha is the best, however it may not be. Not to do myself out of business I would like to suggest you draw up a comparison table of pricing and features. Each and every provider will give you comparison tables or reasons why they are the best, but remember advice will be given based on their viewpoint!

The Plan

Why have a plan?
Who's your audience?
What's the purpose?
List your goals
Timeline
Measuring the results

Why have a plan?

Studies show that if you plan your goals then you are far more likely to achieve them. So in order to achieve email marketing success, you must first write them down somewhere. In a planner, on a white-board or print it out then tack it up for all to see. *Make it official!*

That's not to say you can't learn from previous campaigns and adjust future ones as you go, but starting with a clear outcome in mind is vital.

Things to consider are as follows:

How often are you planning to send out your newsletters?
What day of the week are you going to send out on?
What's the purpose? Why would someone subscribe? What's your expertise?
What holiday hotspots can you ride on? Is there an offer to coincide?
How much time will I dedicate to review my campaign performance?

Starting with this is a great place to begin, and in time you will be tweaking and changing your campaigns to suit your specific readers. So for example, if you send out on a Wednesday and get a 10% open rate, try and send out on a Tuesday, Thursday or even on a weekend to see if your readership goes up or down. Try sending on different times and days, change the design and layout to see what happens.

Marketing isn't a dark art; it's a trial and error game, which differs for each and every business. So enjoy the journey and let us know how you get on at inbox@76uk.com.

Who's your audience?

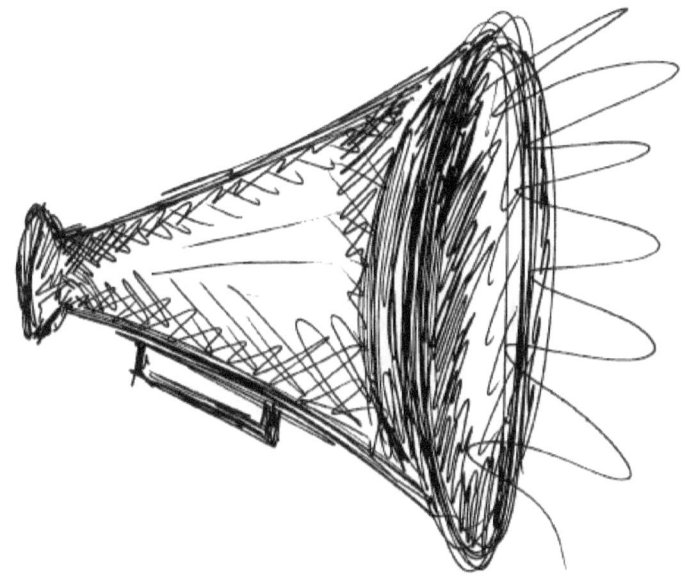

Know your readers. I don't mean physically, although that would be ideal through a focus group, I mean listen to their needs, give them what they want, second guess their requirements and become a trusted source of information.

I watched a TED video* that suggested why Apple are more successful than Dell. The reason was simple; they don't sell features or specs, they sell their vision of the world and where they sit within it, encouraging likeminded folk to join them. *They just happen to sell computers that are good!*

The reason this is important is that you will attract likeminded readers who like your style and opinions, and buy into your dream.

So, my advice is to write as you would talk, write from the heart, write with character, write boldly, don't be afraid to have an opinion. Doing this will attract likeminded people and your writing will flow as its coming freely rather than being forced.

As a return for your efforts you will get to know your readers better, thus making it easier to market your services and products to them because they'll actually be listening to you.

Once you grow your readership, chances are you will have different sets of people liking different things you are talking about. Segmenting your email lists is a great way to do this. You can see click, open, viewing habits, then based on results segment them into new lists. After a while you will have lists for all types of customer. For example; if you sell software online you eventually have multiple lists segmented by habits. One list will be full of online shoppers who like special offers on Microsoft products, you will have another for people who like Apple, another for people who only like your news, not your offers… *so on and so on.*

* http://www.ted.com/talks/simon_sinek_how_great_leaders_inspire_action.html

What's the purpose?

This is a very important one, *don't skip it!*

Do you know why you are sending all these emails? Is it just because you have a list and think you'd better send something? Or do you actually have something valuable to give?

Having purpose in life is what drives us humans to achieve, so why shouldn't other things have one? One of the first words we mutter as a child is the constant WHY WHY WHY WHY? Ask the same of your campaigns. Make them work for you.

So, now we've established that you need to plan your campaigns with military precision, we need to know exactly why you are sending them out. Much like a blog. Starting a blog can be a daunting task, what do you talk about? Why would anyone read it?

Answer these questions:

- ? Why does your business do what it does?
- ? Why bother or care?
- ? What are you passionate about?
- ? Why do you get up each day?

Once you know your business and personal purpose (which with hope should align together) then you will have some idea of the expertise you can share with your readers and become the go-to person for this topic. Plus it will (with hope) align with your brand message and vision.

List your goals

I'm forever writing out lists. Life goals, daily plans, weekly and monthly to-dos. It's how I achieve all the things I want to in life, both personally and in business. If I didn't do this, my brain would fry from overload.

Give your campaigns a purpose, set some goals, list what you hope to achieve by sending them out. It could be as simple as 'we want more subscribers', 'we want more web visitors' or 'we want to sell some special offers' etc etc.

For example, if my purpose were to get more web visitors, I would make sure every line had a hyperlink to my website. If my goal was to sell special offers then I would hit holiday hotspots to piggy-back on.

By listing your goals you are far more likely to achieve them.

Timeline

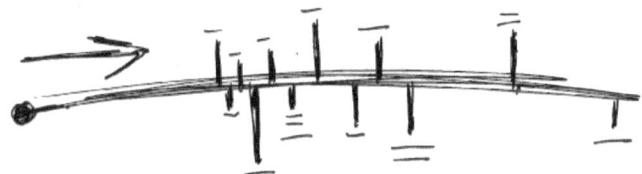

So, hopefully by now you have set out a clear list of goals. Well done. Now lets draw up a timeline of events and dates. A visual map of the 'whats' and 'whens'.

To best see what I mean, here is an example timeline for a fictitious electronics company:

Plan:

- Monthly newsletter
- Created on Friday afternoons
- Sent out on a Saturday at 6am (review and revise month-by-month)
- Monitor for 1 hour on a Monday morning and compare results across campaigns

Campaigns:

- August – summer holidays, sunny images, summer offers (fans and fridges)

- September – new educational year, sell school / learning software
- October – winter's coming… heaters and hot water bottles
- November – black Friday special offer
- December – merry xmas, massive sale now on
- January – January blues, new year new you! Learn and new skill, Wii fit?

Measuring the results

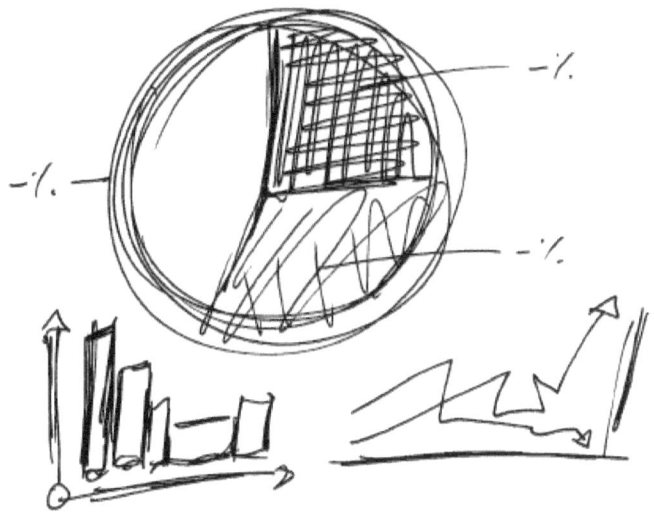

It's one thing to use Google Analytics to track and analyse your website visitors or use social media monitoring tools, but to track the clicks, opens and views of your email campaigns is by far more powerful. By doing this you will get to know your customer's habits more so than any social or web tool can offer.

Every tool worth its salt will offer some in depth level of analysis of your campaigns. After you've sent them out you will be able to see the clicks mount up before your very eyes in real-time. Use this information to fine tune your campaigns, note interesting findings and compare your campaigns performance. Note what you did and would do differently next time.

Learn for the next time!

The right message

Relevance
Spam
Body works
Check it out
Links matter
Sign your name
Subject matters
Pre-headers
Word play
The personal touch
Jargon & buzzwords
Image ready
Attachments
On the go
Holiday hotspots
Track results
Social sync
Hooks
Call to action
The legal stuff

Relevance

According to an online dictionary, the definition of relevant is as follows: Closely connected or appropriate to the matter at hand. Closely connect means that there is a synergy between you, the sender and your readers. Appropriate means that you aren't sending Viagra to children or marketing messages to marketing companies. *Know your audience.*

Every aspect of your email campaigns must compliment and align with your audience. From the aesthetics such as images, colours and fonts, to the very language you use. Your language needs to speak directly to them. *What do your customers want?*

Spam

Up until writing this book I thought SPAM was an acronym, but it turns out it isn't. SPAM is a slang word for unsolicited commercial email. Unsolicited means that the recipient hasn't given you permission to send it.

I'm going to be controversial here, with my personal / business owner hat on, not my Alpha hat… I don't actually think a legitimate enquiry from one business to another is SPAM. Especially if it was sourced via the recipients website.

In America they are very hot on the whole issue of SPAM, and it may look to change that way on this side of the pond too, but for now it isn't.

In this economy we live in, any means to contact and deal with new prospective business partners is a great thing. More of us should be doing it. I encourage it. However the label SPAM has transferred in people's minds into anything they don't fancy reading.

I am passionate about design; I love great logos and typefaces. So a while back I thought about putting a coffee-table book together showcasing creative works, giving each designer a profile with links to their websites and some free promo. I sent an email to a bunch of digital designers from a design directory and sent a lengthy email about my proposal. I received discs in the post from some very keen impoverished artists, but not enough to fill a book. However to coincide with the law of Mr Sod I also got some irate forum posts pasting my entire email proposal and blasting me for ripping off artists work for my own greed. Accusing me of SPAMMING!

In short, when sending your emails out, be extremely careful. There are some people out there who wont think twice before spending a few hours of their not-so busy day trying to destroy your reputation. *Do you want that kind of publicity?*

How can we avoid the junk box?

"There are a number of things involved in getting your email delivered. Some of these are technical in nature, and are best handled by an email marketing service unless, of course, you want to learn how to implement DKIM, process feedback loops, and handle other technical challenges that arise in-house.

The good news is, once you have outsourced those technical issues to an email marketing service, the deliverability-related responsibilities that fall to you are relatively easy.

To get your email delivered, send email that people want, to people who have asked for it and expect it. If you do that, you'll minimize spam complaints, which are a key determinant of whether ISPs put your emails in the inbox or the Junk folder. An added bonus: doing this will maximize not only your delivery rates, but also your response rates.

There are certainly other things you can do, for example: I recommend getting subscribers to add your email address to their address books, but honestly, sending email people want, expect, and have asked for is 95% of what you have to do to get to the inbox."

Justin Premick, AWeber

Body works

When writing your campaign it's important to spend some time on it. The best way is to write it, condense it, proof it, revise it and then preview it. Here goes:

Write it: Write all of the content you want in it, news, events, links, stories, quotes, products etc.

Condense it: Now go at it with a sledgehammer and cut off the fat. Get rid of any fluffy words and make your message as punchy as you can. I mean headlines, links, bullet points, bold fonts and colours…

Proof it: This is important. Don't just hit send! Ask someone nearby to read it. Or better still designate or ask a key recipient of your emails who isn't within your business to preview the email exclusively before anyone else with the view to sending you back some constructive feedback.

Revise it: Take the comments on board and revise your email.

How do I get subscribers?

"Value; there's a perceived cost to every action and a perceived value as well, so you need to be sure you're providing as much value or more value than what people believe to be the cost. So, if I'm going to give up my email address, which for a lot of people is a big deal, don't send me stuff I don't want. You need to match that (value) with something they want — something of value to them. Not just white papers, but something of real interest to them, real research, real data."

Pamela Markey, MecLabs

Check it out

Another point not to be overlooked is checking your campaigns. How they look? Do they make sense? We've all sent emails in haste only to read it later and it either doesn't make sense or the tone is all wrong. The best approach is to write it on day one, proof and preview it on day two, then send it on day three.

Send yourself a copy of your campaigns; preview it in a web browser, read it on your mobile devices (more on that later) as well as your desktop or laptop.

Then, you're good to go… send and wait for the results to pour in!

What testing is important before launching a campaign?

"The most important thing you can test in email -- even before testing subject lines - is the name in the "From" field your prospect sees."

Ben Settle

Links matter

According to a Hubspot study 'The science of effective email marketing' the more links in your email, the more chance people will click through to your website. Although this may be an obvious statement, it is vastly overlooked by email marketers.

It's one thing to plaster headings, paragraphs and bullet points all over your emails, but to turn every few words into hyperlinks will increase your click-throughs by a massive percentage. *Isn't the whole purpose of your campaigns to drive people to a service or product?*

So here's your homework: Go through your latest campaign, then where applicable turn keywords into hyperlinks. The reason I say applicable is that I don't mean to turn every word into a link!

Links in your emails are as vital as the content you've written and the time you send it. *Use links wisely, but use them liberally.*

Sign your name

In most circumstances it's customary but not essential to add a footer signature stating who you are. In email marketing terms it shows you aren't a spammer and you are open to communication.

Compare a spam email to a professional business proposal; what's the difference? Sometimes it is simply the email signature. Spammers don't tend to send a million emails in one go and wait by the phone for annoyed recipients to call!

My signature is as follows:

Happy regards,

Dhugal Dennison
CEO & Co-Founder
<76 logo>
dhugal@76uk.com
+44 (0) xxxx xxx xxx
+44 (0) xxxx xxx xxx
http://76uk.com
http://twitter.com/76uk

76 Applications Limited (Company No: 07651221), 3-5 Wood Street, Old Town, Swindon, SN1 4AN

Try to include as many forms of contact as possible, such as; Skype, phone, email, live chat, Facebook, Twitter, LinkedIn.

Subject matters

A subject line is the shop window of your email, it's your tagline. To not have a catchy subject line is like a newspaper without a headline. Headings and subject lines draw people in.

There are 2 types of subject line for 2 different purposes; first is a marketing email, a one-off mailshot. This will be something like '**50% off Alpha this weekend only**'. The second is a regular email newsletter that people will know as being your regular campaign. This goes something like '**76 News: 31/05/2012**'

Studies show that using a non-salesy subject line means that your regular readers can spot your emails in the 81% of spam they get and may archive it for reference or later reading. This is why great content is so important.

How long should my subject line be?

"My take on it is to do whatever you have to do to get the email opened. If that means a longer subject line, then so be it. Most of my subject lines are five words or less, but that doesn't mean I haven't used 10 or 12 word subject lines. What's more important than length is being pithy. Take out any word that doesn't need to be there.

Every email is different. You have to approach each one as its own entity - so you can see what's worked before, but don't be a slave to any rules. In fact, I enjoy changing things up and breaking rules just for the fun of it. And many times, it pays more than playing it safe."

Ben Settle

Pre-headers

Pre-headers are a relatively new thing. If you have a smart phone you'll have seen a pre-header without knowing it.

A pre-header is a bit of sub-text that welcomes your email, it sits right at the top and in most cases says 'View in browser' or similar. However if you know its prevalence, you can use it as a secondary subject line.

See this example of what a pre-header looks like. Notice most people aren't using it effectively.

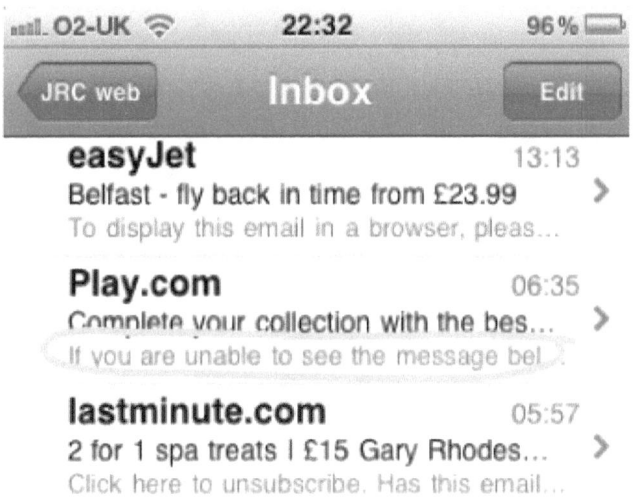

Word play

A study of over 9 billion emails shows the following words are the best words to use in your campaigns to grab attention:

- Apply
- Opportunity
- Demo
- Connect
- Payment
- Conference

Whereas the following are words not to use:

- Free
- Discount
- Offer
- Money

- Confirm
- Join
- Assistance
- Speaker
- Press
- Social
- Invite

Although there is very little actual facts as to why certain words work better than others, we can assume that words such as connect, apply or payment are demanding words that require the recipient to perform an action, whereas words like free and discount are words that suggest giving you something instead.

The personal touch

A little personalisation goes a long way, however don't go over board and use their name, age, sex, location etc to the point of stalker-ish behaviour.

To most recipients, mentioning their dress size may cause alarm and provoke a negative reaction, prompting them to ask where you obtained their data.

The real power of having such data isn't to fill each sentence with personalisation; it's actually to be able to segment your lists into gender, interested, location, profession etc to better target your campaigns.

I personally like having emails addressed to me, but the personal service needs to flow through all aspects of the email, for example using a signature with a personal contact telephone number and from a real person!

Jargon & buzzwords

Jargon when you're selling to someone is an instant death move. Its almost as annoying as hearing business or management speak, listening to deluded business people talk the latest buzz words, or joining an organisation to be bombarded with their internal language just leaves you feeling left out of the loop.

Using 'buzz words' on the flip side can be a benefit in marketing terms. Although cringe worthy to hear, studies show that they actually work if the recipients are familiar with it and place value on them.

As humans we instinctively want to be accepted and be part of a secret club that feels rewarding. Using buzzwords that are 'the latest thing' are of a similar mind-set. You are speaking a language that your eager customers want to hear. *Think of Lady Gaga with her 'little monsters'.*

So, in short; cut the business-speak and create a counter-culture through language and attitude that differentiates you from your rivals. *Think of Apple vs Microsoft.*

Image ready

Believe it or not in this day and age there are a huge number of people who still use plain text (this is non-HTML) emails. According to Jupiter Research, 40% of recipients prefer not to get HTML emails.

So, what happens when you send an HTML only email with large blocks of image rather than lines of text? The 'plain text' readers don't see anything.

Although HTML emails get twice the response rate to plain text emails a survey from 2002 showed that 62% of consumers prefer plain text emails. So what's the best solution? *Cater for both.*

Embedding images into your emails (rather than hosting the image elsewhere and simply displaying by pointing to it from a line of code) is another thing. In your email service provider (ESP), whether it Alpha or Outlook, you can simply paste or insert and image into your emails which makes the overall email size larger.

The other downside is that if an image falls into the spam folder or a setting is ticked to disallow images, your email will look very unprofessional if heavily reliant on images showing up.

My advice? Use an image here and there like your logo or an icon, but focus mainly on links links links, not images images images.

There was a trend a few years back to pack their email with large images, making the whole email look like a postcard or flyer. Thank goodness that designers are now being clever about it and have realised that its better to cater to the masses and not a few people that think their emails are cool.

Do photos and videos in email work?

"If you're going to send an email with images in it, you should host those images on your website and use their URLs to display them in the email. Most email marketing software makes this easy to do.

As for video, most recipients' email programs will not allow video to play directly in the email, so you need to send subscribers somewhere they can watch it online.

The best way to do this is to take a screenshot of the video, put that image in the email, and link the image to the webpage where the video is embedded. That way, subscribers click the video player image and are taken to the video page to watch."

Justin Premick, AWeber

Should you use images in your campaigns?

"A sweeping generalisation but yes, if you have relevant images then you should use them but there is a balance that should be taken into consideration that you don't make the whole email images. Use relevant punchy copy and keep that above the fold. Most email clients wont download images by default and as such if you just rely on the image to make the sale you are restricting your chances."

Mike Parry, Inbox Warriors

Attachments

Personally, I'd say sending attachments in your email campaigns is a big no-no. Not only do they sometimes get caught up in spam filters, but recipients are very wary of attached files for fear of viral contamination.

A better option is to upload the file to a web server or social site. For PDFs or Powerpoints use Slideshare or Scribd, for video use YouTube or Vimeo, for docs use Google docs, for images use Flickr or Photobucket.

Better still, create a page on your website and put a link in the page to the file. This way you have at least fed your subscribers back to your website, which should be one of the sole purposes of your email campaigns.

On the go

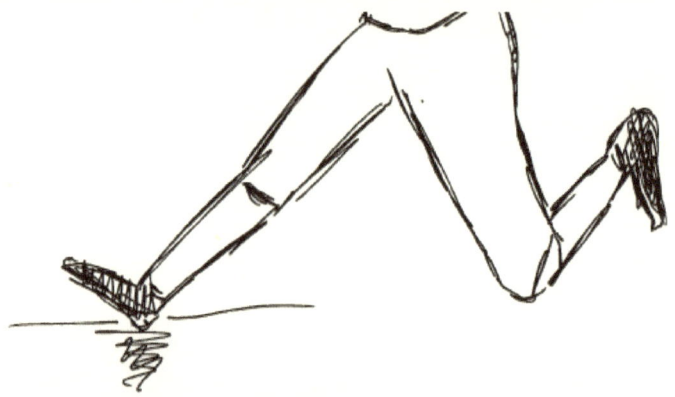

The majority of recipients read their emails on desktop PCs (62%) or on their laptops (23%), however 15% of your audience are reading on the go via mobile and tablet devices. This percentage is growing faster each year.

Fine-tuning your campaigns for mobile view is time well spent. *Think of how your campaign will look all squashed and reduced on a handheld screen.*

A key factor is the width of your email and text size. For cross-platform design its better to use a % width and text size, not fixed point. This means that if someone is reading on their phone, tablet, laptop or desktop they see a similar style throughout.

My advice would be:

- Use fewer images
- Use pre-headers
- Have catchy bold headings
- Have less paragraph text with some bullet points on key parts and as above
- Use % width and % font size

Any designer worth their salt will know what is required here.

Holiday hotspots

Hotspots are key times throughout the year when you seem to get tonnes of emails. Think of Christmas, New Year, Birthdays, Mothers Day, Valentines Day and Halloween, to name a few.

Although it's great to send at these times; a word of caution… don't simply send for the sake of it. Plan a promotional offer for this time. Think of Black Friday.

Send with purpose!

If everyone else is sending at this time it's harder to get your voice heard, but it's also a great time to plan special offers as people both expect to receive marketing messages and have prepared to spend a little extra. *Don't miss out.*

Track results

One of the reason I love email and one of the main factors it is the fastest growing marketing medium (*still*) is that it is trackable. You can view bounces, subscribes, unsubscribes, clicks, browser views, forwards, opens in a way that you can't through mailshots, social media or website analytics. *Plus, it's cost effective too.*

Try A/B split testing for example. You can send out 2 versions of one campaign and depending on which is getting more clicks or views by a certain sending quantity it sends the winning email out to the rest of the list.

In Alpha, like many other services, you can also integrate Google Analytics with your campaigns, meaning if you have Analytics installed on your website and you add links in your campaigns to this website, you can track the clicks locations and habits in Google Analytics much the same way you can with your website stats.

So in a nutshell, to really harness the power of your emails campaigns, you need to track them, gather the results, compare campaigns and tweak them as you go. Over time you will gather a picture of your customer's habits and market to them more effectively.

The key is to see what's working and what's not, then learn from it.

Social sync

It's impossible to ignore social media. It's blown up over the past 10 years or so. It's hard to run a business of any size or nature and not have a presence on either Facebook, Twitter, YouTube or LinkedIn.

With most email sending services you will be able share your campaign on your social accounts, either manually or automatically.

This is a great way to push your campaigns out in a non-intrusive way to your social contacts.

To take this a step further, there are lots of social posting services out there like Ping.fm and Pixelpipe that let you post your links and media across multiple platforms easily for free.

A word of advice here, Its not a great secret but needs stating; social networking is about networking, not blasting (the key is in the word 'social'). To use social networks effectively you must engage in conversations, not simply blast your messages out there.

What's the best way to integrate social with email?

"I use social to grow. I use social to improve the effectiveness of my emails. And essentially, I'm using social to cut costs. If I have social content, essentially what I'm doing is putting social content in my emails. Basically what this does is it drives up my open rates. Now I'm putting something out which is no longer just promotional, it's inspirational and my open rates can go as high as 65% to 75%. Essentially you're showing content is king and user generated content indeed rules."

Sundeep Kapur, Email Yogi

Hooks

A great way to encourage signups to your newsletter is to offer something useful and valuable. A mini-course is a very effective way of achieving this. Mini-courses via email can be considered as blatant marketing ploys and some find them cheesy, however they can be great if produced with care and thought.

Simply gather some of your resources together; web content, articles, blog posts, industry data, videos, facts and stats and collate them into 3-5 simple bite-size emails over a few days or weeks. Produce it once, and then let it fly.

Recipients are getting some great content and you are gaining readership.

An example of a short mini-course would be the following:

1. **Week one**: Offer an overview of your product
2. **Week two**: Give a tour of the key features and benefits
3. **Week three**: Summarise and offer a discount to get started (say 20%)

A word of warning here; if you are planning to add the recipient to your main mailing list as well as send them the requested info, be upfront about it and cover your tracks. You could get some irate emails if you don't tell people upfront.

Call to action

We've covered the power of links in your campaigns, but your whole campaign needs to be full of 'calls to action'. A call to action is something like; click here now, buy this now, sign up today, read more, discover more here…

Whatever the purpose of your campaign, you are undoubtedly trying to funnel your audience towards a destination such as your website, your shop or your blog. According to a study, 68% of readers are hungry for incentives like free guides, prize draws, raffles, downloads or whitepapers. *Feed them!*

The legal stuff

At the bottom of most emails is usually (if they're following the law) a link to "unsubscribe". I've noticed some companies do unsubscribes right, and others... not so much. So heres are my rules that you should always follow for YOUR email list:

1. The best unsubscribe link takes you to a page that says "You've been removed from our list"... and that's it.
2. The second best way (if you really think your email recipients are so stupid they may click it unintentionally) is to have a page with two buttons. One saying "Unsubscribe" and another saying "Oops! I made a mistake!
3. NEVER ask for my email address to unsubscribe. You should KNOW my address.
4. NEVER send an "Unsubscribe Confirmation" email. Seriously? Are you that stupid? I just said "Don't send me any more emails".
5. Do NOT ask me to sign in and "change my notification preferences".

The right time

There are no experts
It's all in the timing
Better days
Watch the frequency

There are no experts

Ignore all experts. Final.

I wrote a blog post some time ago called 'There are no experts', and I stand by this. 'Experts' are in plentiful supply nowadays and the term is mostly self-proclaimed. My gripe is; how can you be an expert in something, in fact anything, that is still evolving and growing and forming new uses and functions in our lives?

Interestingly enough if you ask what most people would badge as an expert they are far more humble. They see themselves on a continuous quest for knowledge and discovery.

Steve Jobs? James Dyson? Mark Zuckerberg? Bill Gates? Tim Berners-Lee? Are they experts? I personally think in each case in a very different way they are geniuses, but experts?

The same rule applies to marketers or email marketers. We launched Alpha about a year ago, but we aren't experts. In fact we are learning each and every day about the rules, howtos, structures etc of email and we are far from knowing it all.

Here at 76 we have some mad ideas as to what and where we can go with email, how far can we stretch and push it. From tracking to sharing to planning to managing, each idea users it in an entirely unique way, but we certainly aren't experts, we are always learning.

It's all in the timing

There's a saying; timing is everything. This is especially true in marketing. Without waffling on, here are the stone cold facts:

62% of people read their emails before 10am, this drops down as the day goes on. In fact, the study of 9 billion emails show us that B2B (business to business) readers want their newsletters sat in their inbox by 6am ready for their morning coffee, at home before the madness of the day ensues. Marketers who scheduled their email campaigns to be delivered between 1am and 5am experienced higher volumes of email opens and clicks. So a rule of thumb is to get it prepared the previous day and schedule it for 1-5am the next morning.

This goes back to the fact that most business people use the same email address for personal and business, and furthermore due to the fact that people's reading habits are changing towards mobile devices. Gone are the days you work 9-5, Monday to Friday.

There's a quagmire of myths surrounding the best timing and it all comes back to your own business and knowing your readers habits through trial and error.

Remember this: People subscribe to your emails, not businesses. So it's more about when they read their emails, not their trading hours. If your average reader works in a large corporate, they will probably check mid-mornings, if your readers are self employed then get it to them early.

Random fact: 42% of social media users check personal email accounts 4 or more times per day, compared to 26% of non social users.

Better days

It goes without saying that some holidays are better than others to send out campaigns on. Christmas day wouldn't be a great day for starters. Individual days of the week make a huge difference too. In the interest of getting down to the facts, here goes:

Day	Send?	Why?
Monday	No	Start of the new week
Tuesday	Hmm	Better than on Monday!
Wednesday	Yes	Best day/s for larger companies
Thursday	Yes	*See above*
Friday	No	People finish early
Saturday	Yes	Best day/s for smaller companies
Sunday	Yes	*See above*

Random fact: Sundays generated the highest volume of opens (12.2%) and clicks (4.4%) on average when compared to the rest of the week.

Watch the frequency

54% of people who unsubscribe from permission-based emails said the reason was emails coming too frequently. This was second to people who unsubscribe because they found the content repetitive or boring (49%).

However don't confuse this with consistency. If someone signs up to weekly newsletter they want a newsletter weekly right? If you start sending every day then they may get annoyed. The only rule is to be honest and upfront about the frequency of your emails, then subscribers know the deal and can't complain.

A study of 9 billion emails suggested it really doesn't matter how often you send emails out, but subscribers just need to be aware. *The key is consistency.*

How frequently should I send?

"You don't want to overload and bombard people with more messages than they are willing to take because you'll get the immediate unsubscribe. At the same time, you don't want to just show up when you have something to sell or promote. What you want to do is hit them with periodic "cookie content" – stuff they look forward to and they are rewarded for opening (with) good solid content. Then when you do have something to promote, they will be responsive because you've earned the right to sell them."

Brian Clarke, Copyblogger

The right people

Buying friends
Scraping up
Opt-in VS double opt-in
The right way
Smart segments

The email checklist

Buying friends

64% of email marketing said that the biggest factor in improving email deliverability was having clean up-to-date email lists, followed by relevance at 52% and sender reputation at 42%.

Note: clean up-to-date email lists, not just email lists. There are loads of email data sellers online, some legit and some not so. It can be hard to know which is which. If unsure, don't buy the data.

Fans of Asimov's 3 rules of robotics are now treated to the 3 laws of buying data:

Golden rule #1
Make sure the data is opt-in and the seller is reputable

Golden rule #2
Don't add the entire database to your mailing list; they need to opt-in

Golden rule #3
If unsure; don't buy, build

Scraping up

Search for email data scraping and tonnes of tools come up. This is big business. Data scraping is the process of using a 'bot' to go out and gather data, usually emails, URLs, addresses and names, and usually results in spammers sending out bogus offers, malware and Viagra sales!

I don't need to be the one to tell you, but this is not a great idea. In fact it's illegal in most cases.

Again… relevance is key. How can an offer be relevant when you don't know the first thing about the person you are sending the email to?

Opt-in VS double opt-in

You've probably heard email marketers use the term "opt-in". This means that messages are sent only upon the recipient's permission. Others talk about "double opt-in" (or "confirmed opt-in") as if it was a completely different matter. But is it?

The Difference Between Opt-In and Double Opt-In

Email addresses on a (single) opt-in list are not confirmed. Anybody can submit anybody's address to the list, and it will be there until it is unsubscribed.

On a double opt-in list, all email address must be confirmed before they are added. A request for confirmation is sent to the submitted address and the address owner must take some action to confirm that

- He / she is the owner of the email address
- The address is working and…
- He / she indeed wants to subscribe

Most often, the confirmation action is as simple as replying to the confirmation request or clicking on a link.

The right way

As if I need to be the one to tell you but the best way to get the best response to your campaigns is to know the people you're sending them out to.

A general rule of thumb is to collate contacts where you can. However there are some unwritten rules here. Most people find the following acceptable when being 'added' to an email list:

- **You don't know someone** = don't contact unless it's a legit enquiry

- **You did business with someone over 6 months ago** – connect on LinkedIn, then ask if they would like to get your emails
- **You attend a business network event and share a business card** = send a short 'hello' email the following day or within a few days
- **You are in business or have close business relations** = add them to your newsletter
- **You are a close friend** = anything goes (within reason)

There are many scenarios however be warned. Spam - and the awareness of the legal aspects of it are becoming more popular as email marketing is becoming more popular. *Be careful out there!*

Have you seen any particularly successful email marketing campaigns and why were they so successful?

"Richer Sounds, www.richersounds.com are regularly our most successful email broadcasting campaigns having particularly high open rates and click rates. They have a good relationship with their data, they capture all their data themselves either instore or siteside, they keep the file very clean, they have a low bounce rate, they send relevant targeted offers and they are consistent with their send times and dates."

Mike Parry, Inbox Warriors

What are the best ways to get email subscribers?

1. "Make it easy for me to give you my email address
2. Run competitions
3. Social sharing
4. Pop up email sign up prompts."

Mike Parry, Inbox Warriors

Smart segments

It's a good idea as you grow and learn through your campaign responses to segment your email lists into smaller chunks. This is great as you can see a particular habit - then in most service providers – auto-segment the people who performed that habit into a new list.

Intelligent online marketers know that there is a powerful technique to reach the right people with the right message at the right time. The technique is segmentation.

Segmentation is the process of creating sub-sets of a target audience made up of people or organizations with one or more shared characteristics. Segmenting your email opt-in list can provide a treasure trove of information that can help you increase your response rates, convert more prospects to sales, and generate add-on, repeat or higher value sales.

Is it worthwhile doing list clean ups, by removing in-active subscribers?

"Yes, in-active subscribers can cause a number of issues,

1. There is a cost implication of mailing them
2. They could contain SPAM traps, which in turn will get you blocked by the ISP
3. They will drag your user engagement %s down which in turn will impact your delivery."

Mike Parry, Inbox Warriors

The email checklist

So, we've gone through loads of do's and don'ts, some advice and tips, so I hope by now you are ready to put your campaign together and start marketing? Hold your horses, here is a quick checklist in no particular order:

- ? Are you sending at the right time and day?
- ? Do the links work and are they correct?
- ? Is there a plain text version?
- ? Is there an unsubscribe button?
- ? Is there a way to track results?
- ? Does it work on mobile devices?
- ? Is there a signature?
- ? Is there a pre-header?
- ? Have you proofed and previewed it?
- ? Are all recipients opted-in?

We hope you like this book, let us know how you got on and give us some feedback…

inbox@76uk.com

Can you share some B2B email best practices?

"Here is a quick checklist. See how you rank on all these, and use the results to develop a plan to refresh and update your email program. You'll quickly see higher results.

1. Focus on the subscriber. Mail less frequently but with more value in each message. Tailor messages to the behaviour (e.g. recent download) or demographics
2. Track your sender reputation and inbox placement rate. If you don't get this data from your ESP today, ask for it
3. Make it easy to see what the call to action is
4. Keep it simple – no one has time to read a lengthy newsletter, even if the content is interesting. Break it up into shorter, pithier messages and guide subscribers to the website
5. Get permission and actively engage to ensure that subscribers still want to be in your file
6. Use a Preference Centre to give subscribers choices, then communicate that they can visit the Preference Center frequently as their needs change
7. Treat prospects differently from customers. Use unique content and a slower pace
8. Highlight and nurture your most active and most socially networked subscribers. Email and social marketing are natural allies. Use them together to build relationships and encourage dialog
9. Carefully vet the sources of your email file – e.g. are some partners sending data that turns out to be unresponsive?
10. Include links to your LinkedIn profile and other social network sites, and encourage subscribers to "Share this" by

providing auto-status update links at each article or call to action."

Are there email practices to avoid?

"Avoid high frequency. Avoid all image-HTML messages (your subscribers will see a big grey box instead of your call to action). Avoid lots of links and images if you think your audience is reading email on mobile devices. Avoid generic messages. Avoid sharing lists between brands or companies – treat the permission grant with respect.

The Golden Rule of email marketing is to treat your subscribers the way you would like to be treated – only sending them information that is relevant, timely and helpful."

Stephanie Miller

Shameless plug

About Alpha
About 76

About Alpha

What is Alpha?
Alpha is an email newsletter-marketing tool. You signup, create your lists, import your subscribers and then start creating your campaigns. You can create from scratch, use one of our ready-made templates or get coding your own designs in seconds.

How does it work?
Alpha is web-based, meaning you have nothing to install and there are no compatibility issues to consider. Simply signup and start marketing.

How much does it cost?
Alpha is competitively priced in the market, so you can be sure of getting the best price across all of the most popular services. Plans cost from 16p per day.

Questions?
help@joinalpha.com

Visit:
http://joinalpha.com

About 76

Born in England, UK on 1st December 2010, 76 was created to fulfil a long running passion for web 2.0, apps, mobile, tech, innovation, ideas and above all... a frustration that some things just don't do what you want them to (hence our switch from a PC to a Mac)!

Dhugal Dennison set up 76 Applications Limited after many years as a web designer (not developer). When the app market exploded a few years back Dhugal decided to start brainstorming some cool apps. Through adult learning and self-exploration Dhugal decided to close his design business, go back underground, read lots of books and re-think the future. This was to design and create apps. This then became 76.

The next chapter of this story involves you. *Join us!*

Visit:
http://76uk.com

http://joinalpha.com

www.ingramcontent.com/pod-product-compliance
Lightning Source LLC
Chambersburg PA
CBHW030842180526
45163CB00004B/1424